THE NEWBIES

BIBLE ALPHABETS
A-Z

By: Barbara Denise Hendricks

Los Newbies

Alfabetos de la Biblia
A-Z

Balboa Press books may be ordered through booksellers or by contacting:

Balboa Press
A Division of Hay House
1663 Liberty Drive
Bloomington, IN 47403
www.balboapress.com
1 (877) 407-4847

Because of the dynamic nature of the Internet, any web addresses or links contained in this book may have changed since publication and may no longer be valid. The views expressed in this work are solely those of the author and do not necessarily reflect the views of the publisher, and the publisher hereby disclaims any responsibility for them.

Any people depicted in stock imagery provided by Thinkstock are models, and such images are being used for illustrative purposes only. Certain stock imagery © Thinkstock.

ISBN: 978-1-4525-1739-1 (sc)
ISBN: 978-1-4525-1740-7 (e)

Library of Congress Control Number: 2014913744

Print information available on the last page.

Balboa Press rev. date: 9/2/2015

BALBOA.
PRESS
A DIVISION OF HAY HOUSE

ABOUT THE AUTHOR

I, Barbara D. Hendricks, am a writer and the owner of Broader Horizons Childcare & Development Inc. I have owned my own daycare and fostered children for 20 years and counting. I wanted to create a whole new children's story series that I could read to my newest grandchildren. When they were born, GOD spoke to me and told me to write a children's book series. I felt as if I have a new transformed life. I thought "what if I could write a whole new book series and read to them?" This children's book series is important to me because it reminds me of how much I love to teach children. In my spare time I help educate families on how to restore their credit.

ABEL

"The Lord respects **ABEL** offering..." *Genesis 4:4 KJV*

ABEL

*"El Señor **ABEL** ofreciendo respeto…"* Génesis 4:4 KJV

B b

BAPTIZE

"**BAPTIZE** you with water unto repentance…" *Matthew 3:11 KJV*

BAUTIZO

*"OS **BAUTIZO** con agua á arrepentimiento…"* Mateo 3:11 KJV

Cc

COMMANDMENT

"These are the **COMMANDMENTS,** which the Lord commanded Moses for the children of Israel in Mount Sinai." *Leviticus 27:34 NIV*

C ch

MANDAMIENTOS

*"Éstos son los **MANDAMIENTOS**, que el Señor mandó (ordenó) a Moisés para los niños de Israel en Monte Sinaí."* Leviticus 27:34 NIV

Dd

DISCIPLE

"If you hold to my teachings, you are really my **DISCIPLES**..." *John 8:31-32 NIV*

Dd

DISCÍPULOS

"Si cumple con mis enseñanzas, son realmente
mis **DISCÍPULOS**... " John 8:31-32 NIV

ETERNAL

"Your word, Lord, is **ETERNAL**; it stands firm
in the heavens." *Psalm 119:89 NIV*

ETERNA

"Su palabra, Señor, es **ETERNA**; se mantiene firme en el cielo." Salmo 119:89 NIV

FAITH

"O ye of little **FAITH**…" *Matthew 6:30 KJV*

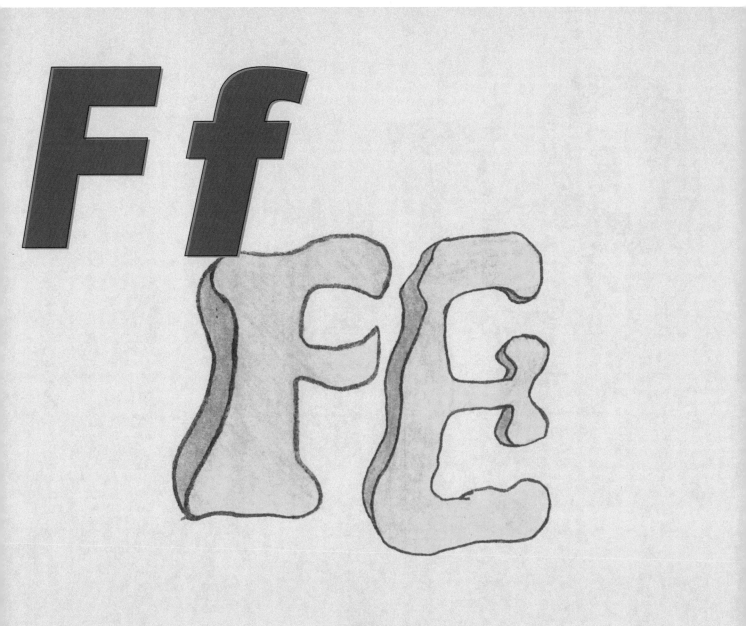

FE

*"O ustedes de poca **FE**…"* Mateo 6:30 KJV

GOD

"Blessed be the most high **GOD**..." *Genesis 14:20 KJV*

G g

DIOS

*"Bendito ser **DIOS** más alto…"* Génesis 14:20 KJV

HEAVEN

"In the beginning God created the **HEAVEN**
and the earth." *Genesis 1:1 KJV*

CIELOS

*"En el principio creó Dios los **CIELOS**
y la tierra."* Génesis 1:1 KJV

Ii

INTEGRITY

"As for you, if you walk before me in **INTEGRITY**..." *1 Kings 9:4 NIV*

INTEGRIDAD

*"En cuanto a usted, si no anda antes de mí en la **INTEGRIDAD**..."* 1 Reyes 9:4 NIV

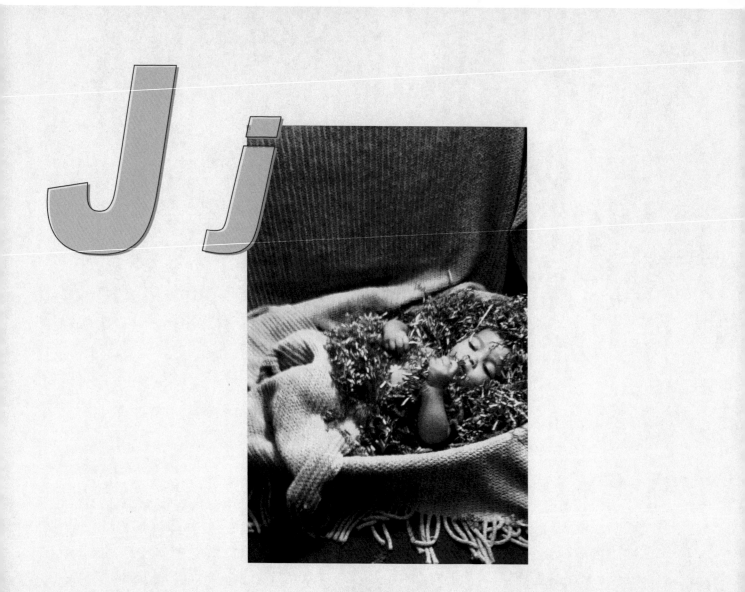

JESUS

"In the beginning of the gospel about **JESUS**
Christ, the son of God." *Mark 1:1 NIV*

JESUCRISTO

"Al principio del evangelio sobre **JESUCRISTO**, el hijo de Dios." *Mark 1:1 NIV*

K k

KING

"KING of **KINGS…"** *1 Timothy 6:15 KJV*

Kk

REY

*"**REY** de **REYES** ..."* 1 Timothy 6:15 KJV

LEADER

"LEADER to people..." *Isaiah 55:4 KJV*

LÍDER

*"**LÍDER** a la gente…"* Isaiah 55:4 KJV

MINISTER

"Elisha **MINISTER** to Elijah…" *2 Kings 19:21 KJV*

M m

MINISTRO

*"**MINISTRO** de Elisha a Elijah..."* 2 Reyes 19:21 KJV

NATION

"An Holy **NATION**…" *Exodus 19:6 KJV*

NACIÓN

"Una **NACIÓN** Santa…" Éxodo 19:6 KJV

OFFERING

"Remember thy **OFFERING**…" *Psalm 20:3 KJV*

OFRECE

"Recuerde thy que **OFRECE**..." Salmo 20:3 KJV

P p

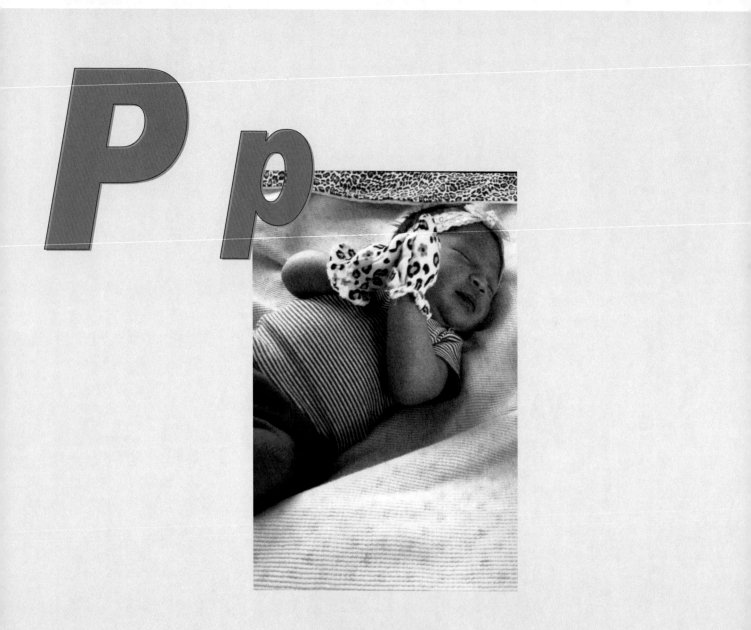

PRAISE

*"Singing **PRAISES**…" Judges 5:3 KJV*

P p

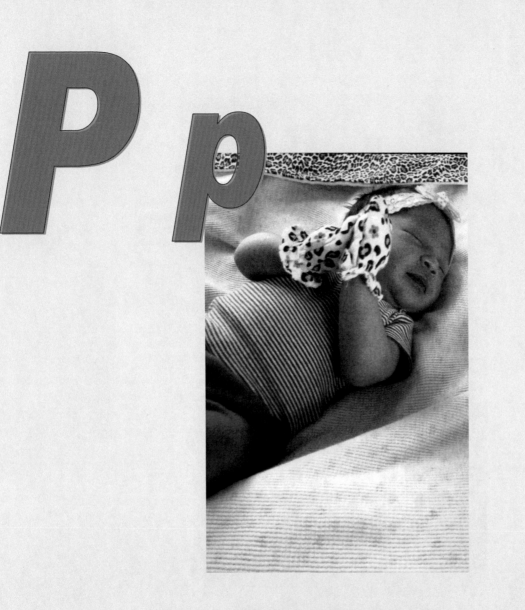

ALABANZAS

"Cantando **ALABANZAS**…" Jueces 5:3 KJV

QUEEN

"QUEEN Esther…" *Esther 7:1 KJV*

REINA

*"La **REINA** Esther…" Esther 7:1 KJV*

REPENT

"REPENT of sin…" *Matthew 3:2 KJV*

Rrr

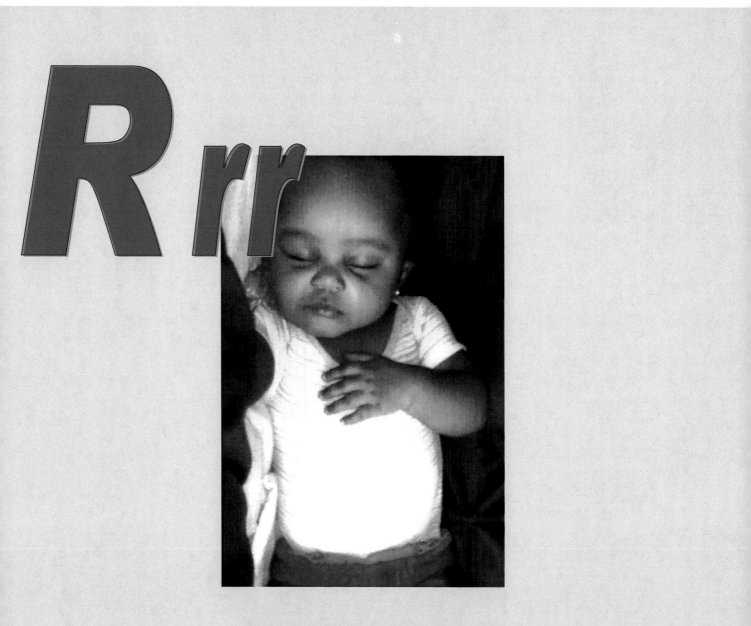

ARREPENTIRSE

*"**ARREPENTIRSE** del pecado…"* Mateo 3:2 KJV

Ss

SAVE

"**SAVE** your soul…" James 1:21 KJV

SALVA

*"**SALVA** tu alma..."* Santiago 1:21 KJV

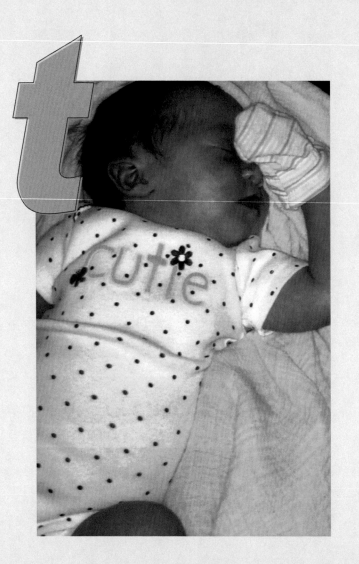

TEMPTATION

"Lead us not into **TEMPTATION**…" *Matthew 6:13 KJV*

T t

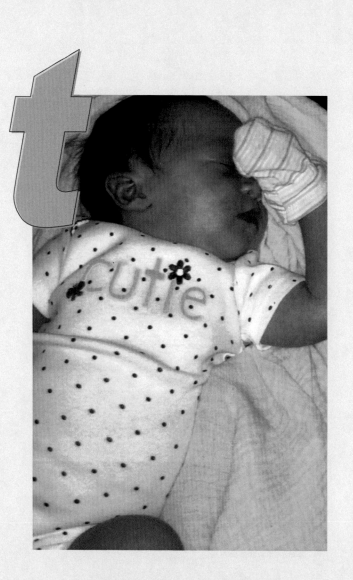

TENTACIÓN

*"Llévenos no a **TENTACIÓN**…"* Mateo 6:13 KJV

UNCLEAN

*"An **UNCLEAN** soul…" Leviticus 5:2 KJV*

U u

SUCIA

*"Un alma **SUCIA**…" Leviticus 5:2 KJV*

Vv

VOW

"When you make a **VOW** to God, do not delay
to fulfill it…" *Ecclesiastes 5:4 NIV*

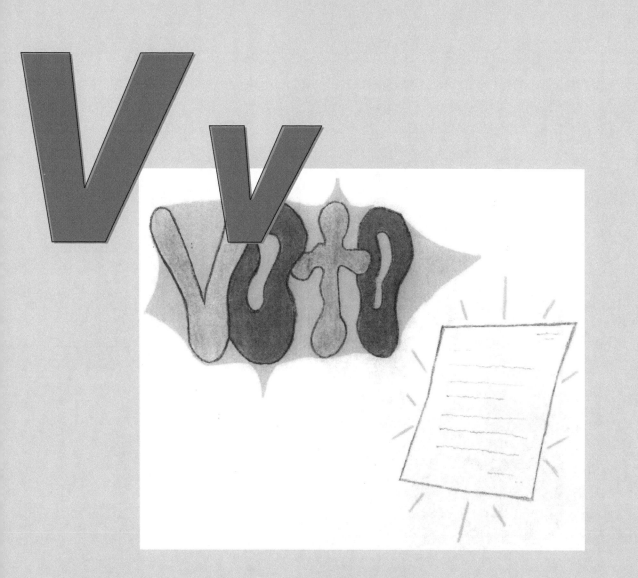

VOTO

*"Cuando haces un **VOTO** a Dios, no se demore para cumplirla..." Eclesiastés 5:4 NIV*

WISDOM

"Glory and **WISDOM**..." *Revelation 7:12 KJV*

SABIDURÍA

"Gloria y **SABIDURÍA**…" Revelación 7:12 KJV

XERXES

"XERXES loved Esther more than any other women…" *Esther 2:17 CEV*

XERXES

"XERXES *amó a Esther más que cualquier otra mujer…"* Esther 2:17 CEV

Y y

YOKE

"Take my **YOKE** upon you, and learn of me..." *Matthew 11:29-30 KJV*

Y y

YUGO

*"Tome mi **YUGO** sobre usted y aprenda de mí…"* Mateo 11:29-30 KJV

ZEAL

"Have a ZEAL of God…" *Romans 10:2 KJV*

CELO

*"Tienen un **celo** de Dios..."* Romanos 10:2 KJV

Thank you God for The Alphabets. In the name of Jesus.
We love you. Amen.

*Gracias Dios por el Alfabetos. En el nombre de Jesús.
Te amamos. Amén.*

Look Out for the rest of the Newbies Series coming soon.

Para el resto de los novatos de proxima aparicion.

Barbara D Hendricks is a writer and the owner of Broader Horizons Childcare and Development Inc. Barbara has owned her own daycare for 20 years. She wanted to create a whole new children's book series that she could read to her new grandchildren and others. When they were born, God spoke to her and told her to write a children's book series. Barbara felt as if she had a new transformed life. Barbara D. Hendricks lives in Chicago, Illinois. She is a mother of four, a grandmother of 14 and counting, and a Godmother of one. Children inspired her book.

Co Author *Denise A.L. Hendricks* is a loving and caring mother of 2. Denise loves helping others, and is a lifetime Girl Scout of Girl Scouts of Greater Chicago and Northwest Indiana. Denise loves traveling, helping her community, and spending time with her family and children. Denise's favorite thing to do is read. Together Denise and her family love reading all different kinds of books.

Editor- *April M. Hendricks* is a loving, caring wife and mother of 7. April has a degree in Healthcare Administration and loves helping others. April enjoys skin care and is an Esthetician. April loves traveling, shopping, spending time with family and friends, and enjoys taking her children to the library for reading time.

Illustrator- *Cory C. Hendricks* loves going to the gym and staying physically fit. Cory loves to stay healthy and draw on his spare time. Cory loves to read books to his many nieces and nephews.

Paris- *London A.A. Van* is a happy and healthy baby girl that loves to shop, travel, visit new places, and meet new friends. London loves to go out and throw on her shades, on hot sunny days, and have plenty fun in the sun. London loves spending time with her siblings; her favorite thing to do is read books with her family.

Jay- *Marcus J.D. Love* is a healthy energetic bouncing baby boy that loves to spend most of his time outside, at the park, and going on road trips with his family. Marcus loves bedtime and story time with his parents and little sister. Marcus favorite thing to do is sit in his reading corner and look at his picture books.

Gabbie- *Marissa M.G. Love* is a lovable baby girl that loves to play with her older brother Marcus. Marissa loves to listen to all the different stories during story time. Marissa favorite thing to do is cuddle with her family and read all kinds of books.

Printed in the United States
By Bookmasters